PIANO • VOCAL • GUITAR

W9-BMT-958

THE DISNEY COLLECTION

Best-loved Songs From Disney Movies,

Television Shows and Theme Parks

ISBN 0-7935-0832-0

HAL•LEONARD®
CORPORATION
7777 W. BLUEMOUND RD. P.O. BOX 13819 MILWAUKEE, WI 53213

THE DISNEY COLLECTION

Alphabetical Listing

The Disney Collection

This listing matches the sequence of the songs on the three recorded albums of THE DISNEY COLLECTION, released by Walt Disney Records and available in your local record stores.

VOLUME 1

VOLUME 2

VOLUME 3

BABY MINE
(From Walt Disney's "DUMBO")

Words by NED WASHINGTON
Music by FRANK CHURCHILL

Moderately Slow

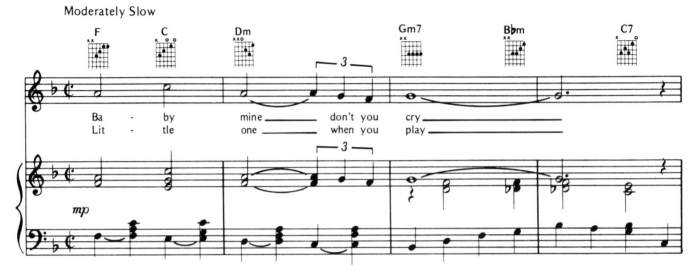

Ba - by mine _____ don't you cry _____
Lit - tle one _____ when you play _____

Ba - by mine _____ dry your eye _____
Don't you mind _____ what you say _____

Rest your head close to my heart, Nev - er to part, Ba - by of
Let those eyes spar - kle and shine, Nev - er a tear, Ba - by of

5

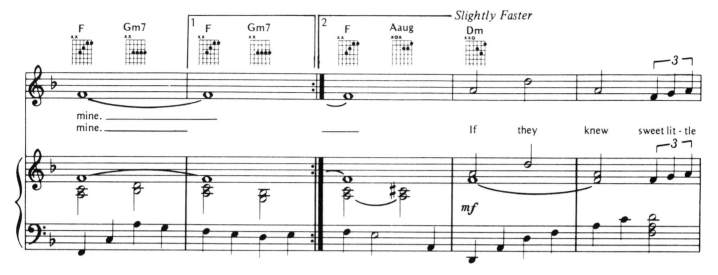

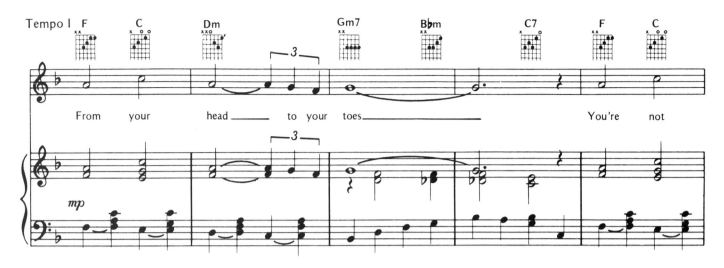

From your head _____ to your toes _____ You're not

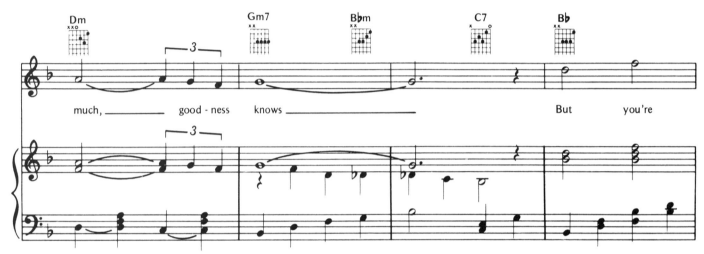

much, _____ good-ness knows _____ But you're

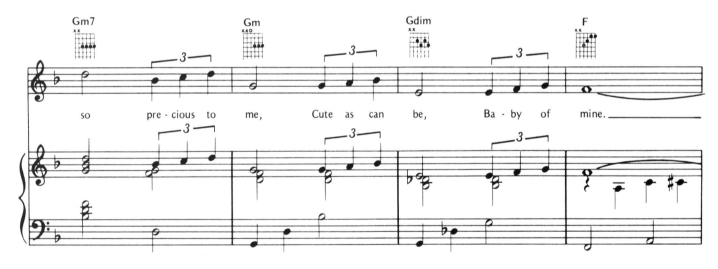

so pre-cious to me, Cute as can be, Ba-by of mine. _____

diminuendo

pp

THE BALLAD OF DAVY CROCKETT

Words by TOM BLACKBURN
Music by GEORGE BRUNS

BEST OF FRIENDS
(From Walt Disney's "THE FOX AND THE HOUND")

Words by STAN FIDEL
Music by RICHARD JOHNSTON

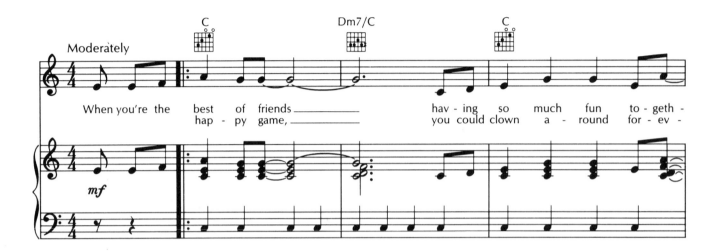

When you're the best of friends _____ hav-ing so much fun to-geth-

hap-py game, _____ you could clown a-round for-ev-

-er, you're not e-ven a-ware ___ you're such a fun-ny pair. ___

-er. Nei-ther one of you sees ___ your nat-ur'l bound-a-ries. ___

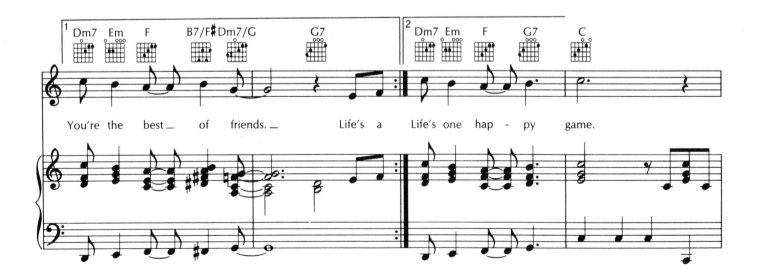

You're the best ___ of friends. ___ Life's a Life's one hap-py game.

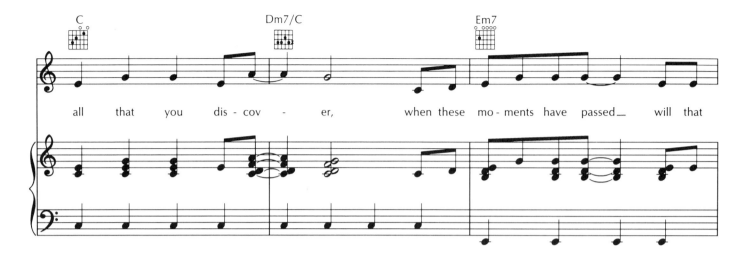

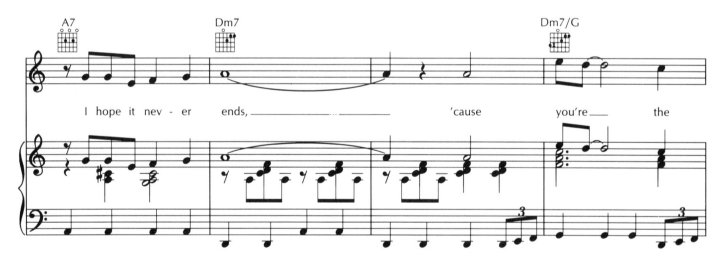

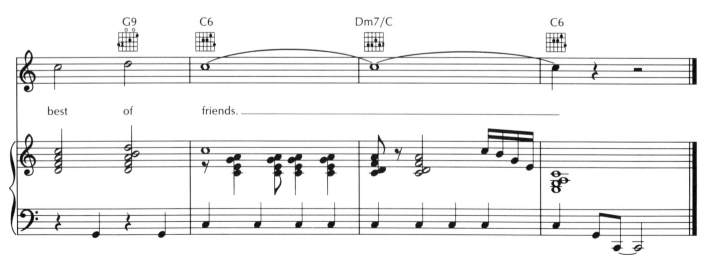

CANDLE ON THE WATER

(From Walt Disney Productions' "PETE'S DRAGON")

Words and Music by AL KASHA
and JOEL HIRSCHHORN

I'll be your can-dle on the wa-ter,
My love for you will al-ways

I'll be your can-dle on the wa-ter,
'Til ev-'ry wave is warm and

burn. I know you're lost and drift-ing, But the clouds are lift-ing,

bright, My soul is there be-side you, Let this can-dle guide you

don't give up you have some-where to turn.

soon you'll see a gold-en stream of

light.

CASEY JUNIOR

(From Walt Disney's "DUMBO")

Words by NED WASHINGTON
Music by FRANK CHURCHILL

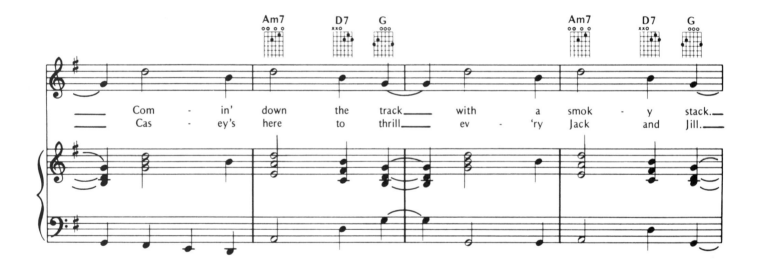

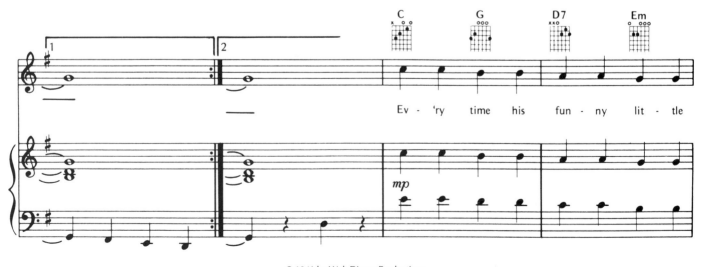

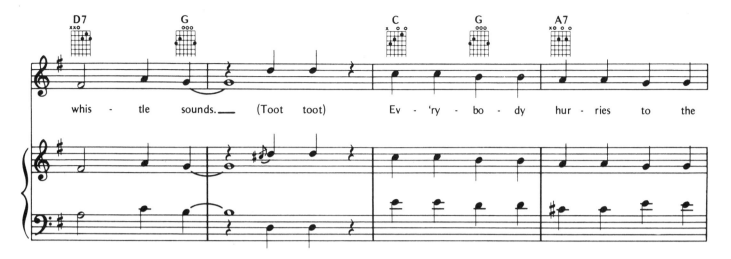

whis - tle sounds.___ (Toot toot) Ev - 'ry - bo - dy hur - ries to the

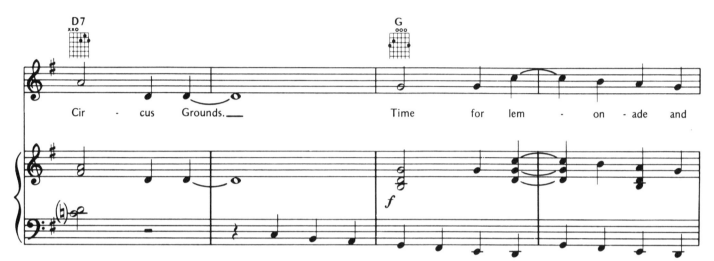

Cir - cus Grounds.___ Time for lem - on - ade and

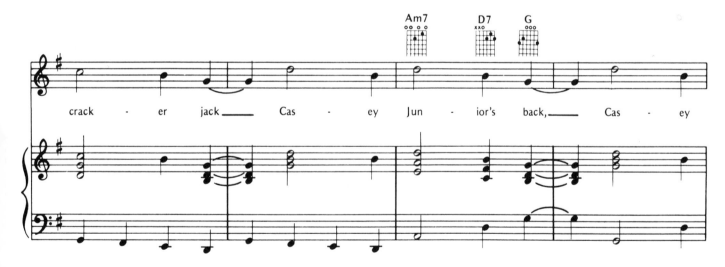

crack - er jack___ Cas - ey Jun - ior's back,___ Cas - ey

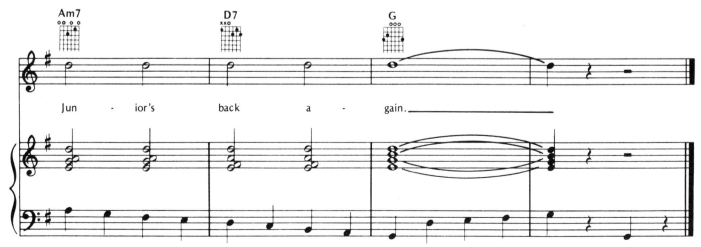

Jun - ior's back a - gain._____

CHIM CHIM CHER-EE

(From Walt Disney's "MARY POPPINS")

Words and Music by
RICHARD M. SHERMAN
and ROBERT B. SHERMAN

27

CRUELLA DE VIL
(From Walt Disney's "ONE HUNDRED AND ONE DALMATIONS")

Words and Music by
MEL LEVEN

A DREAM IS A WISH YOUR HEART MAKES

(From Walt Disney's "CINDERELLA")

Words and Music by MACK DAVID,
AL HOFFMAN and JERRY LIVINGSTON

EV'RYBODY WANTS TO BE A CAT
(From Walt Disney's "THE ARISTOCATS")

Words by FLOYD HUDDLESTON
Music by AL RINKER

35

Come on, scat cat, turn me on,_ I'll take my horn and my best tone,_ Then blow a lit - tle soul in - to the

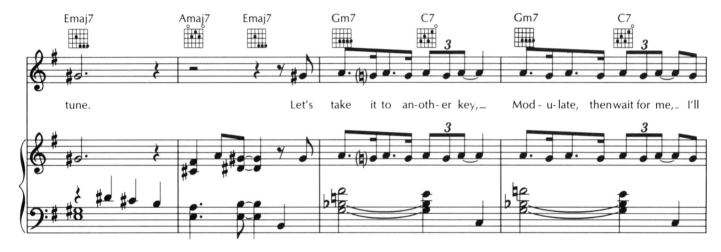

tune.   Let's take it to an - oth - er key,_ Mod - u - late, then wait for me,_ I'll

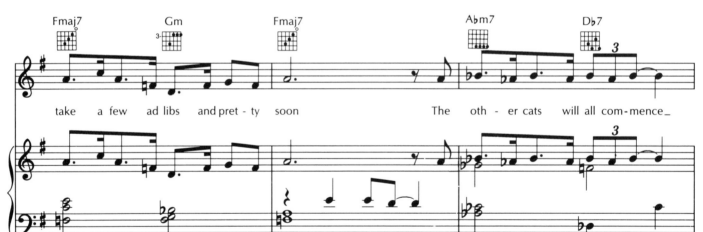

take a few ad libs and pret - ty soon   The oth - er cats   will all com - mence_

D.C. al Fine

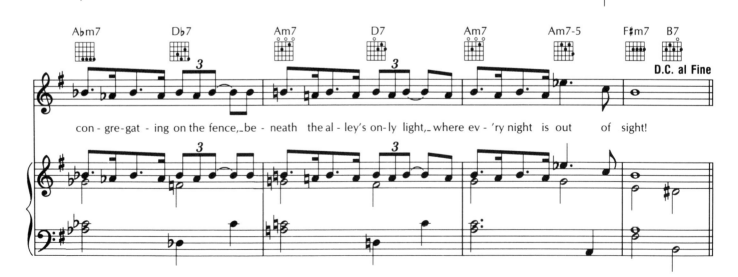

con - gre - gat - ing on the fence,_ be - neath the al - ley's on - ly light,_ where ev - 'ry night is out   of sight!

FEED THE BIRDS
(From Walt Disney's "MARY POPPINS")

Words and Music by RICHARD M. SHERMAN
and ROBERT B. SHERMAN

Ear- ly each day to the steps of Saint Paul's the lit - tle old

bird wo - man comes. _____ In her own spe - cial

way to the peo - ple she calls, "Come, buy my

Tempo I

Though _____ her words are sim - ple _____ and few,

lis - ten, _____ lis - ten, _____ she's call - ing to you:

"Feed _____ the birds, tup - pence _____ a bag,

tup - pence, _____ tup - pence, _____ tup - pence _____ a bag."

FOLLOWING THE LEADER

(From Walt Disney's "PETER PAN")

Words by TED SEARS and WINSTON HIBLER
Music by OLIVER WALLACE

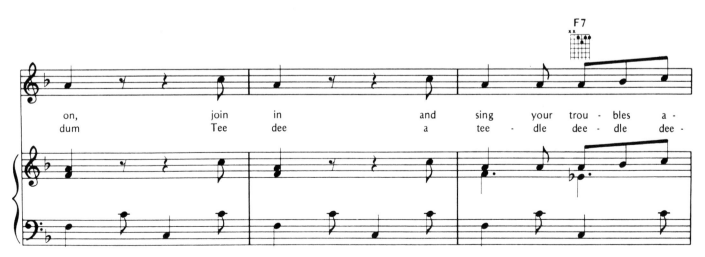

way with a tee - dle ee dum a tee - dle ee dō tee
ay, oh, a tee - dle ee dum a tee - dle ee dō tee

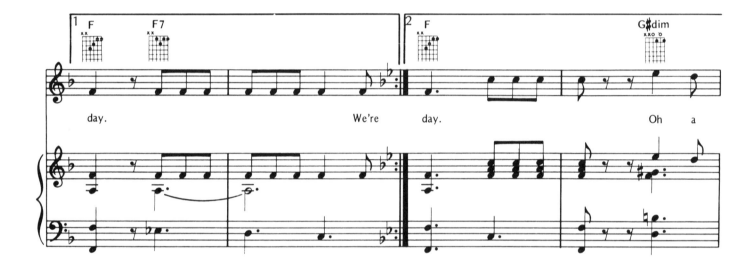

day. We're day. Oh a

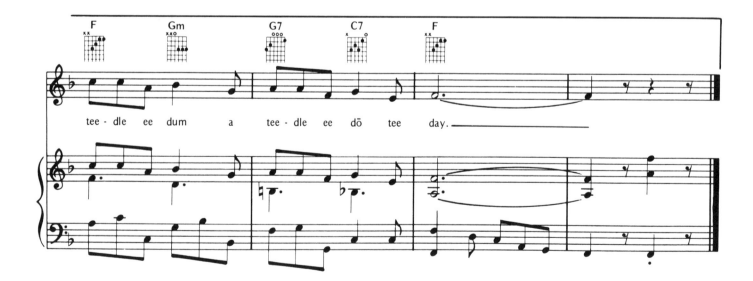

tee - dle ee dum a tee - dle ee dō tee day.

I WAN'NA BE LIKE YOU
(From Walt Disney's "THE JUNGLE BOOK")

Words and Music by RICHARD M. SHERMAN
and ROBERT B. SHERMAN

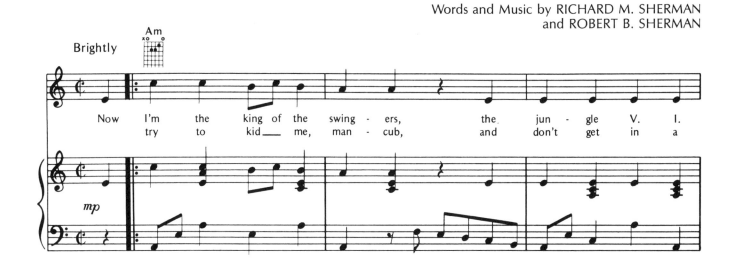

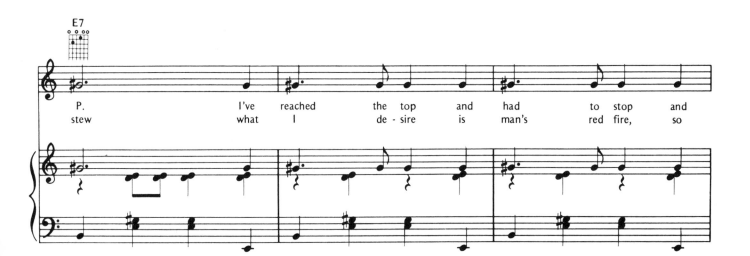

man - cub, And stroll right in - to town, and
man - cub, Just clue me what to do,

be just like the oth - er men, I'm tired of mon - key - in'
me the pow'r of man's red flow'r, and make of my dream___ come

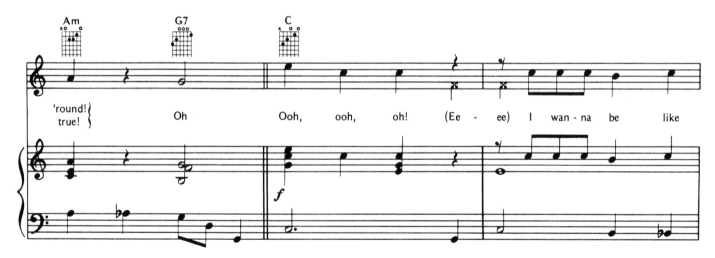

'round! } Oh Ooh, ooh, oh! (Ee - ee) I wan - na be like
true! }

you, ooh, ooh! (Ee - ee) I wan - na walk like you,

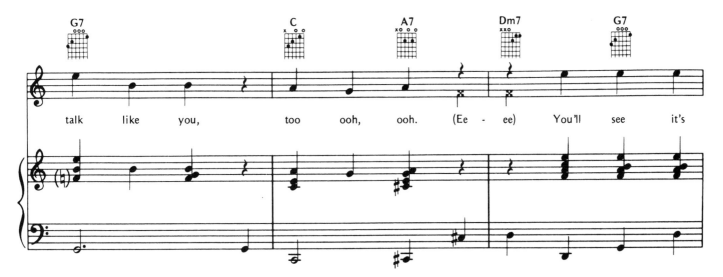

talk   like   you,   too ooh,   ooh.   (Ee - ee)   You'll   see   it's

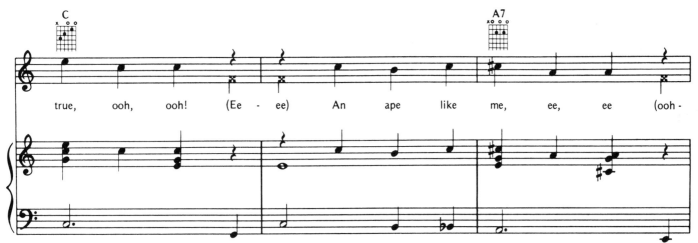

true,   ooh,   ooh!   (Ee - ee)   An   ape   like   me,   ee,   ee   (ooh -

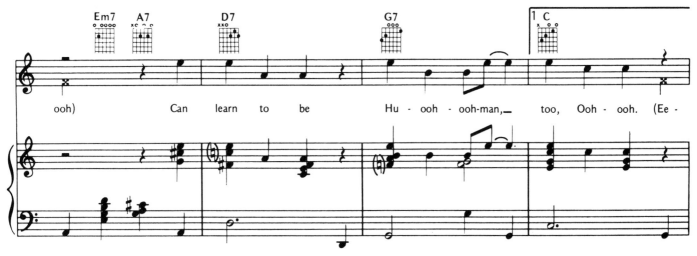

ooh)   Can   learn   to   be   Hu - ooh - ooh-man,___   too,   Ooh - ooh.   (Ee -

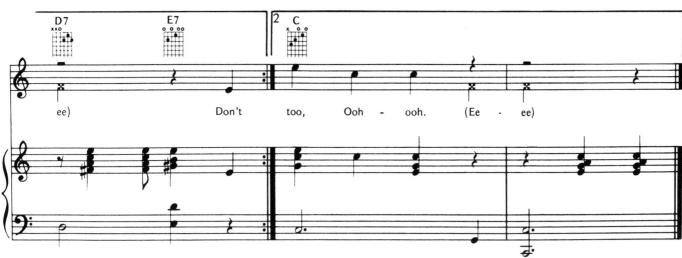

ee)   Don't   too,   Ooh - ooh.   (Ee - ee)

GIVE A LITTLE WHISTLE
(From "PINOCCHIO")

Words by NED WASHINGTON
Music by LEIGH HARLINE

When you get in trou-ble and you don't know right from wrong;
When you meet temp-ta-tion, and the urge is ver-y strong; } Give a lit-tle

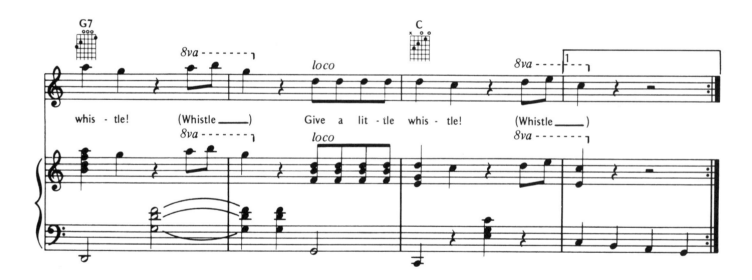

whis-tle! (Whistle ____) Give a lit-tle whis-tle! (Whistle ____)

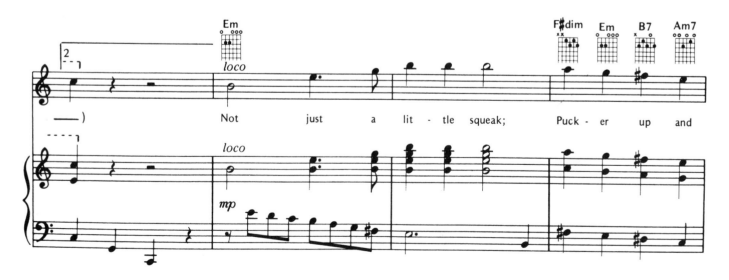

____) Not just a lit-tle squeak; Puck-er up and

HE'S A TRAMP
(From Walt Disney's "LADY AND THE TRAMP")

Words and Music by PEGGY LEE
and SONNY BURKE

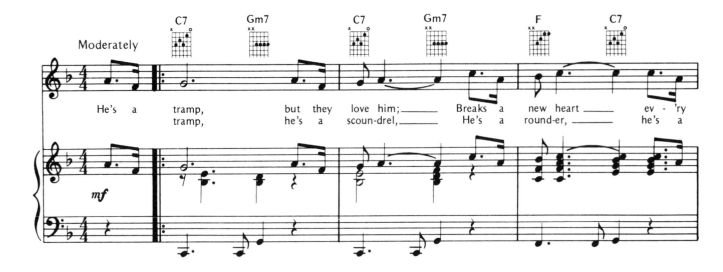

He's a tramp, but they love him; Breaks a new heart ev-'ry
tramp, he's a scoun-drel, He's a round-er, he's a

day. He's a tramp; they a-dore him And I on-ly hope he'll stay that
cad, He's a tramp, but I love him. Yes,

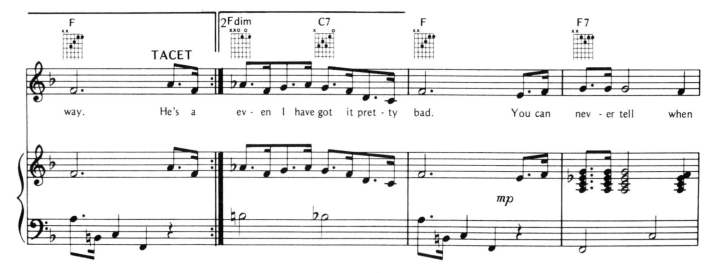

way. He's a even I have got it pret-ty bad. You can nev-er tell when

he'll show up; He gives you plen-ty of trou - ble. I guess he's just a

no 'count pup, __ But I wish that he were dou-ble. He's a tramp, he's a

rov - er __ And there's noth-ing more to say. __ If he's a tramp, he's a

good one __ And I wish that I could trav-el his way. __

8va
lower

HEIGH-HO
(THE DWARFS' MARCHING SONG from "SNOW WHITE AND THE SEVEN DWARFS")

Words by LARRY MOREY
Music by FRANK CHURCHILL

Bright and Cheerful

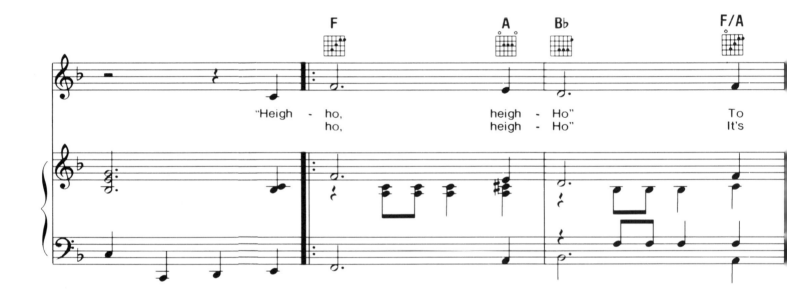

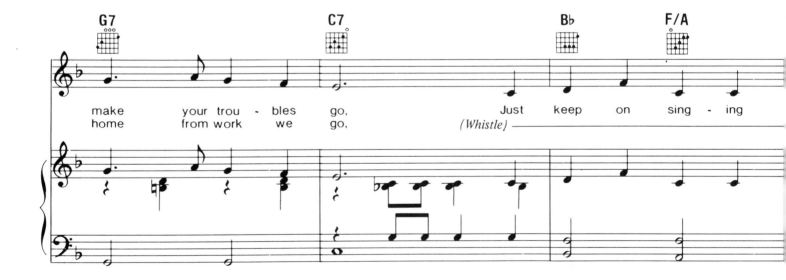

HI-DIDDLE-DEE-DEE
(An Actor's Life For Me)
(From Walt Disney's "PINOCCHIO")

Words by NED WASHINGTON
Music by LEIGH HARLINE

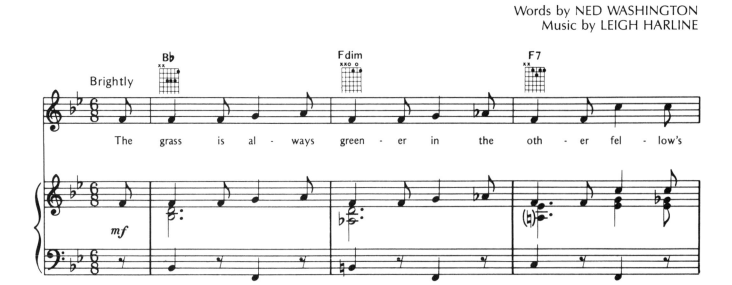

The grass is al-ways green-er in the oth-er fel-low's

yard.___ No mat-ter what your life may be you think your life is

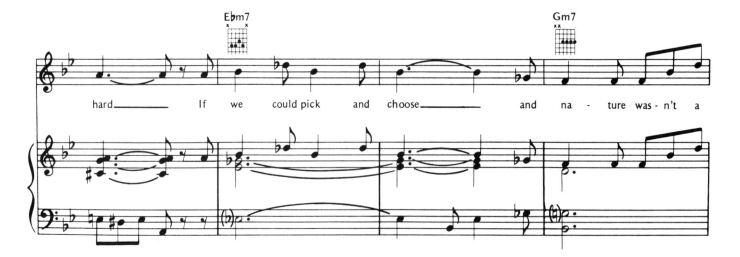

hard___ If we could pick and choose___ and na-ture was-n't a

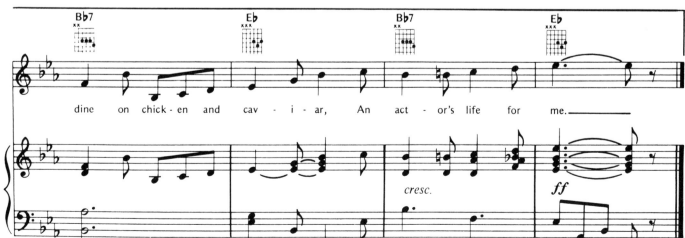

I'VE GOT NO STRINGS
(From "PINOCCHIO")

Words by NED WASHINGTON
Music by LEIGH HARLINE

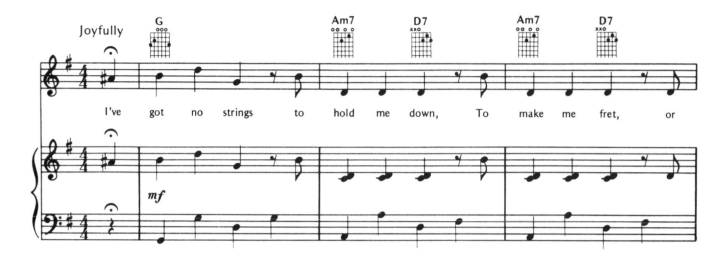

I've got no strings to hold me down, To make me fret, or

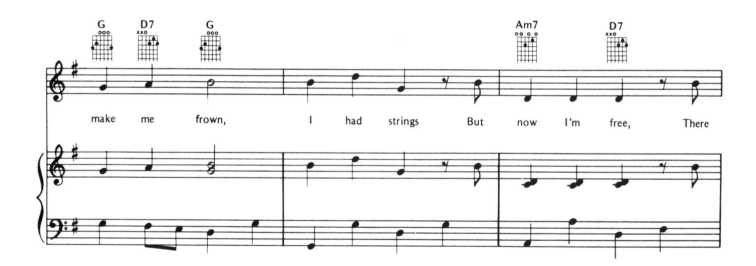

make me frown, I had strings But now I'm free, There

are no strings on me. Hi o the

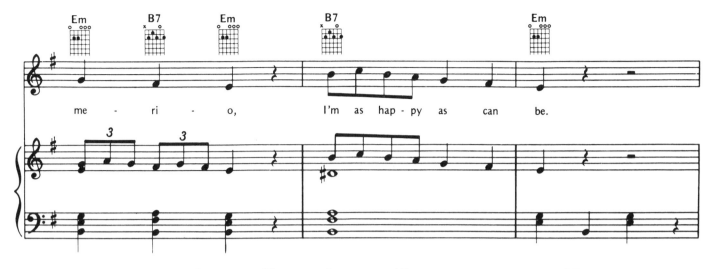

me - ri - o, I'm as hap - py as can be.

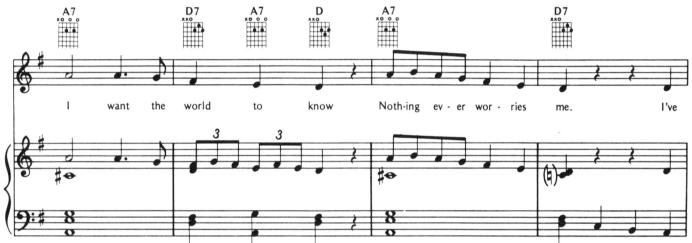

I want the world to know Noth-ing ev - er wor - ries me. I've

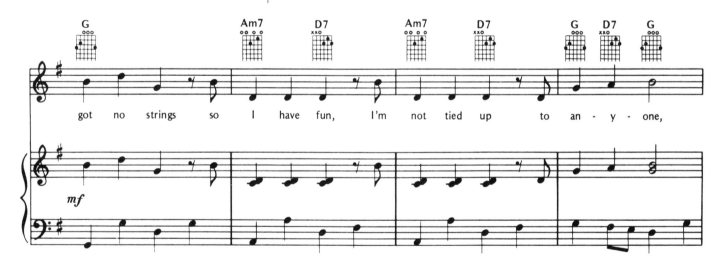

got no strings so I have fun, I'm not tied up to an - y - one,

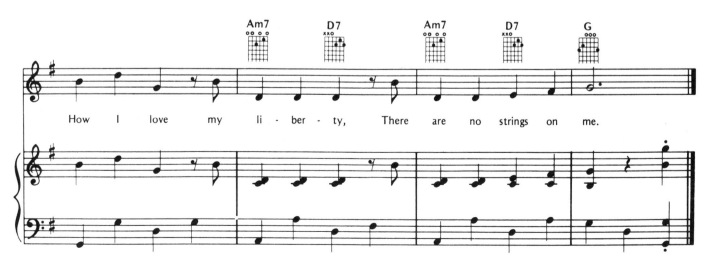

How I love my li - ber - ty, There are no strings on me.

I WONDER
(From Walt Disney's "SLEEPING BEAUTY")

Words by WINSTON HIBLER and TED SEARS
Music by GEORGE BRUNS (Adapted From Tschaikowsky Theme)

Moderately, with a swing

IT'S A SMALL WORLD

(Theme from The Disneyland and Walt Disney World Attraction, "IT'S A SMALL WORLD")

Words and Music by RICHARD M. SHERMAN
AND ROBERT B. SHERMAN

March Tempo

It's a world of laugh - ter, a world of
just one moon and one gold - en

63

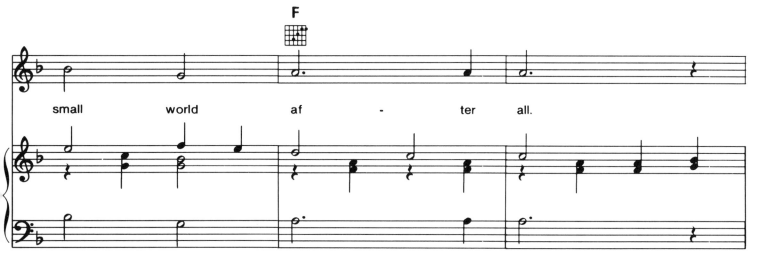

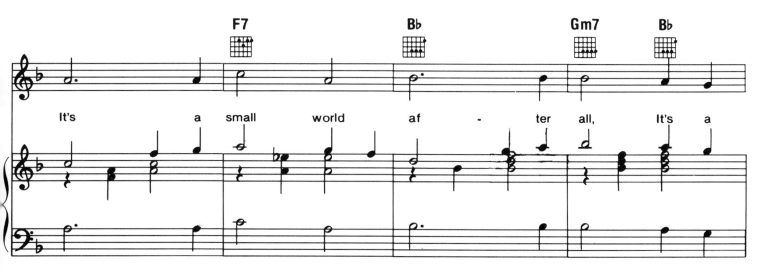

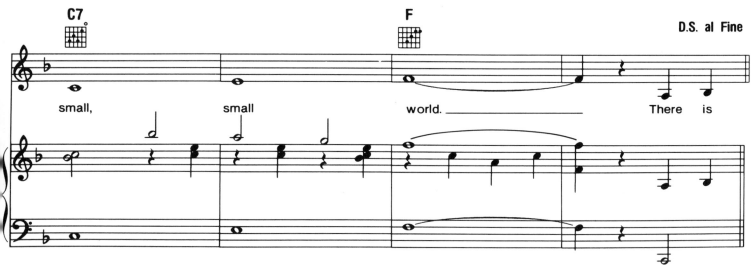

JOLLY HOLIDAY
(From Walt Disney's "MARY POPPINS")

Words and Music by RICHARD M. SHERMAN
and ROBERT B. SHERMAN

66

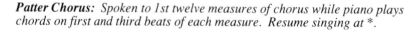

Patter Chorus: Spoken to 1st twelve measures of chorus while piano plays chords on first and third beats of each measure. Resume singing at *.

BERT: Mavis and Sybil 'ave ways that are winning
And Prudence and Gwendolyn set your 'eart spinning;
Phoebe's delightful, Maude is disarming,
Janice, Felicia, Lydia, charming;
Winifred's dashing, Vivian's sweet,
Stephanies's smashing, Priscilla a treat;
Veronica, Millicent, Agnes and Jane,
Convivial company, time and again;
Dorcas and Phyllis and Glynis are sorts,
I'll agree are three jolly good sports,
But cream of the crop, tip of the top,
It's Mary Poppins, and there I stop!

KISS THE GIRL
(From Walt Disney's "THE LITTLE MERMAID")

Lyrics by HOWARD ASHMAN
Music by ALAN MENKEN

don't know why, _ but you're dy-ing to try. You wan-na kiss the girl.

Yes, you want __ her.

Look at her, you know you do. __ Pos-si-ble she wants you, too.

__ There is one __ way to ask her. It don't

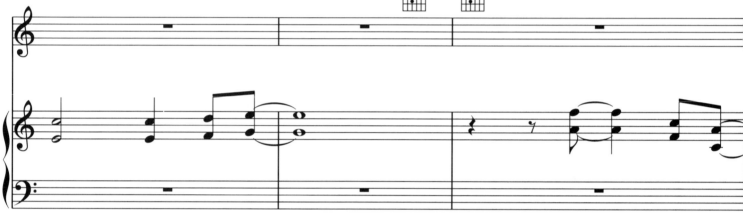

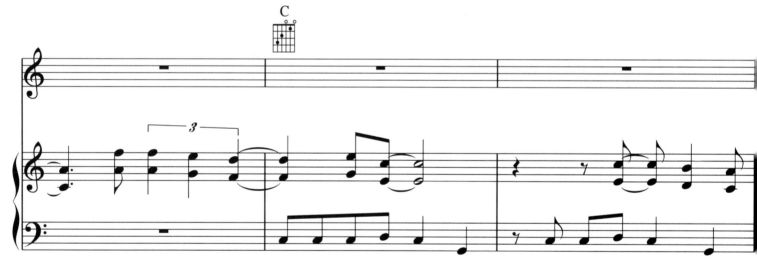

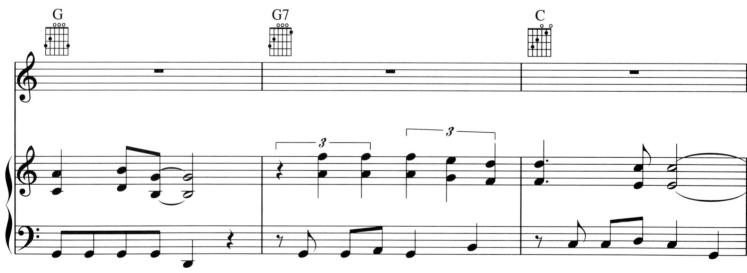

73

LET'S GO FLY A KITE
(From Walt Disney's "MARY POPPINS")

Words and Music by RICHARD M. SHERMAN
and ROBERT B. SHERMAN

LITTLE APRIL SHOWER
(From Walt Disney's "BAMBI")

Words by LARRY MOREY
Music by FRANK CHURCHILL

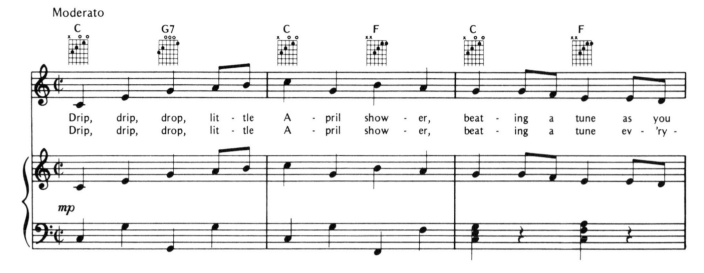

Moderato

Drip, drip, drop, lit-tle A-pril show-er, beat-ing a tune as you
Drip, drip, drop, lit-tle A-pril show-er, beat-ing a tune ev-'ry-

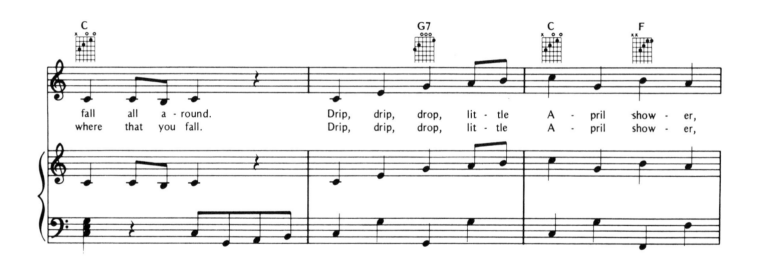

fall all a-round.   Drip, drip, drop, lit-tle A-pril show-er,
where that you fall.   Drip, drip, drop, lit-tle A-pril show-er,

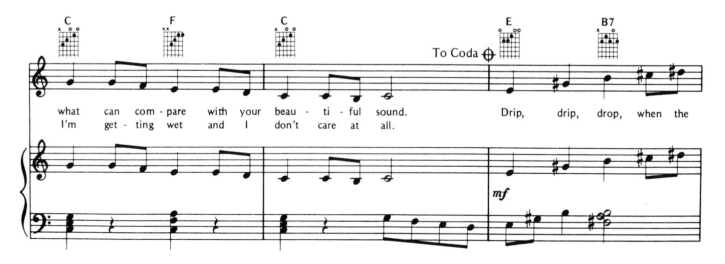

what can com-pare with your beau-ti-ful sound.   Drip, drip, drop, when the
I'm get-ting wet and I don't care at all.

To Coda

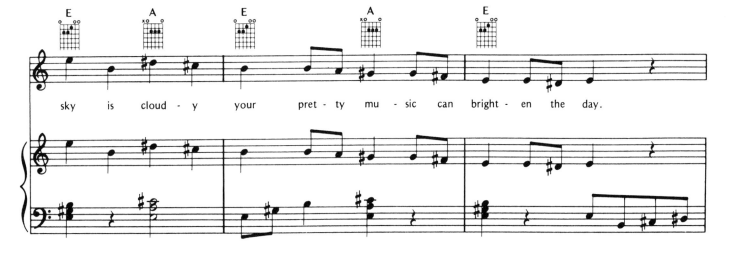

sky is cloud - y your pret - ty mu - sic can bright - en the day.

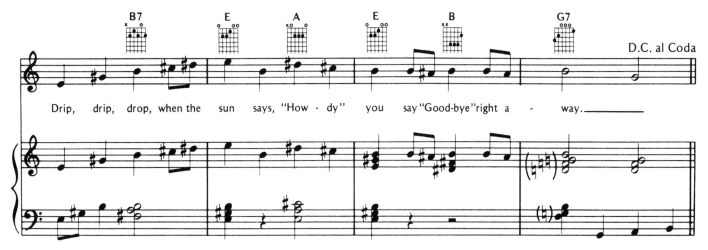

Drip, drip, drop, when the sun says, "How - dy" you say "Good-bye" right a - way.____

D.C. al Coda

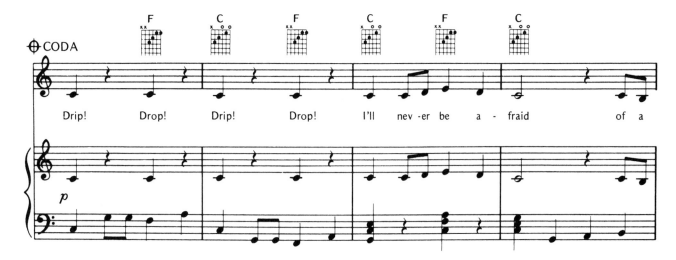

CODA

Drip! Drop! Drip! Drop! I'll nev - er be a - fraid of a

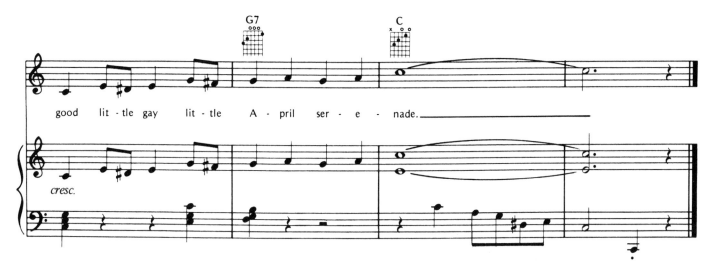

good lit - tle gay lit - tle A - pril ser - e - nade.____

LOVE IS A SONG
(From Walt Disney's "BAMBI")

Words by LARRY MOREY
Music by FRANK CHURCHILL

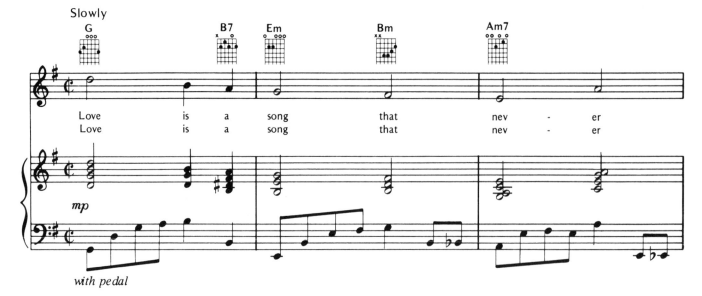

Love is a song that nev - er
Love is a song that nev - er

ends. Life may be swift and
ends. One sim - ple theme re -

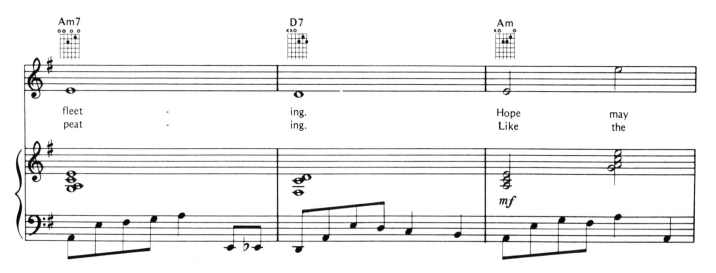

fleet - ing. Hope may
peat - ing. Like the

81

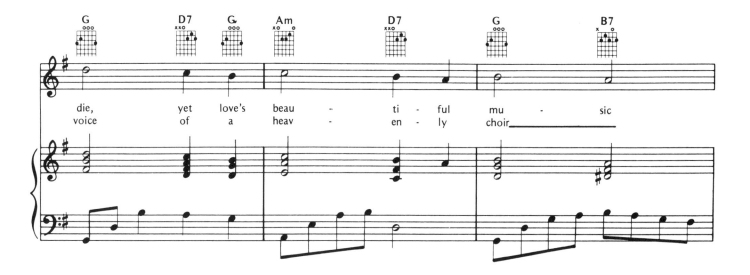

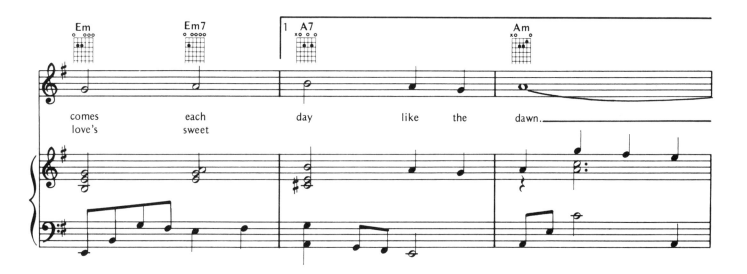

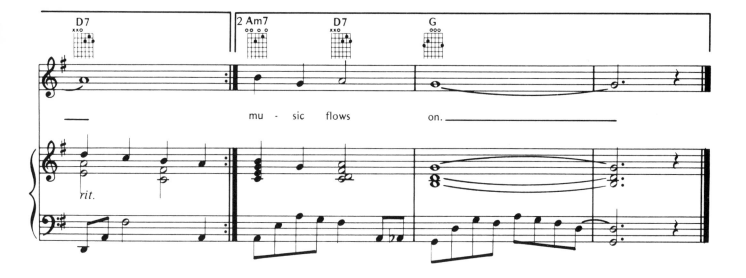

MICKEY MOUSE MARCH

Words and Music by
JIMMIE DODD

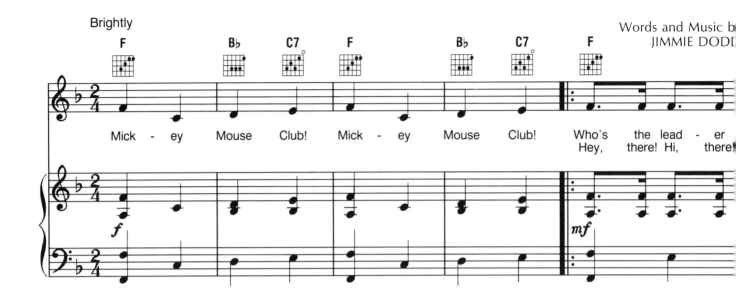

Brightly

Mick - ey Mouse Club! Mick - ey Mouse Club! Who's the lead - er
Hey, there! Hi, there!

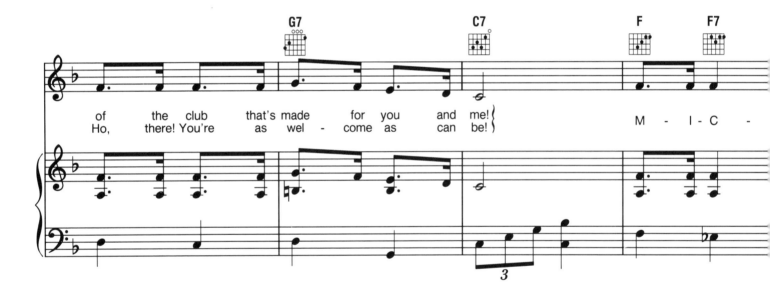

of the club that's made for you and me!
Ho, there! You're as wel - come as can be!

M - I - C -

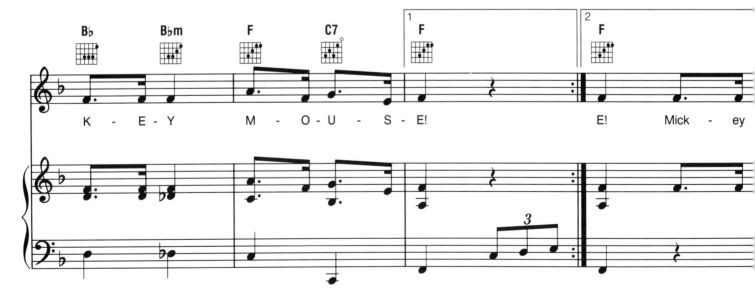

K - E - Y   M - O - U - S - E!

E!   Mick - ey

MICKEY MOUSE ALMA MATER

(From Walt Disney's TV Series "MICKEY MOUSE CLUB")

Words and Music b
JIMMIE DODD

85

ONCE UPON A DREAM
(From Walt Disney's "SLEEPING BEAUTY")

Words and Music by SAMMY FAIN
and JACK LAWRENCE

I know you! I walked with you once up-on a

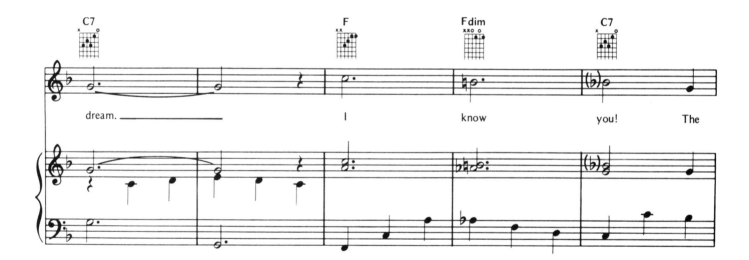

dream. _____ I know you! The

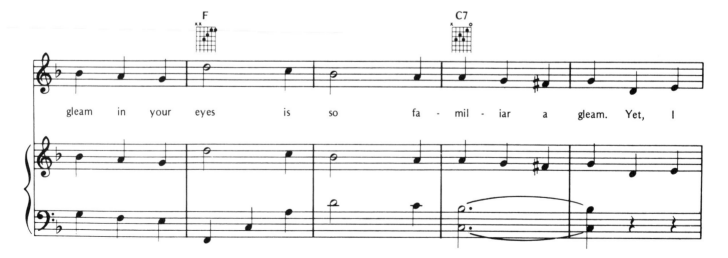

gleam in your eyes is so fa-mil-iar a gleam. Yet, I

know   it's   true   that   vi - sions   are   sel - dom

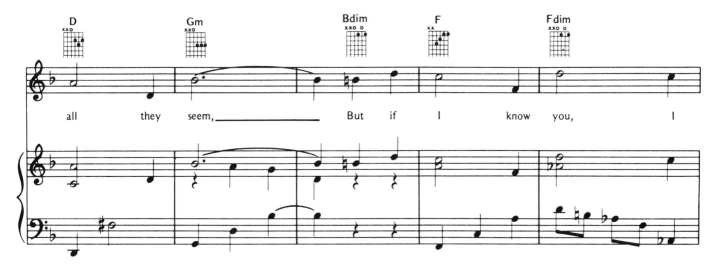

all   they   seem,_____   But   if   I   know   you,   I

know   what   you'll   do;   You'll   love   me   at   once   the   way   you   did

once   up - on   a   dream._____

ONE SONG
(From Walt Disney's "SNOW WHITE AND THE SEVEN DWARFS")

Words by LARRY MOREY
Music by FRANK CHURCHILL

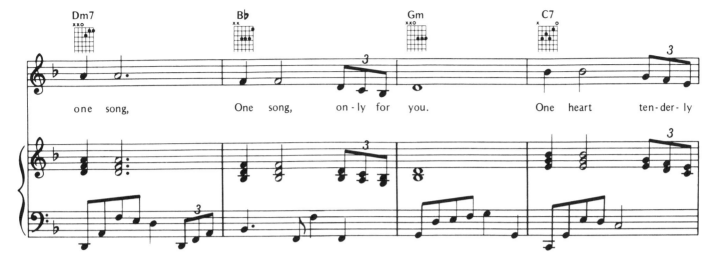

one song,　　　One song,　on-ly for you.　　　One heart　ten-der-ly

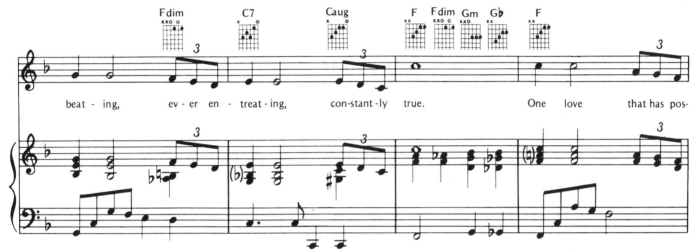

beat - ing,　ev - er en - treat - ing,　con-stant-ly true.　　　One love　that has pos-

sessed me,　　　One love,　thrill-ing me through,　　　One song,　my heart keeps

sing - ing　　of　one love,　on -ly for you.　　　you.

PART OF YOUR WORLD

Lyrics by HOWARD ASHMAN
Music by ALAN MENKEN

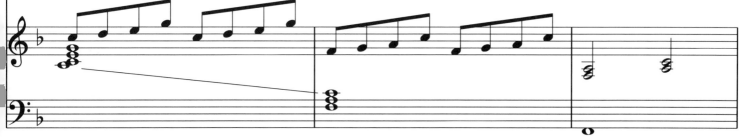

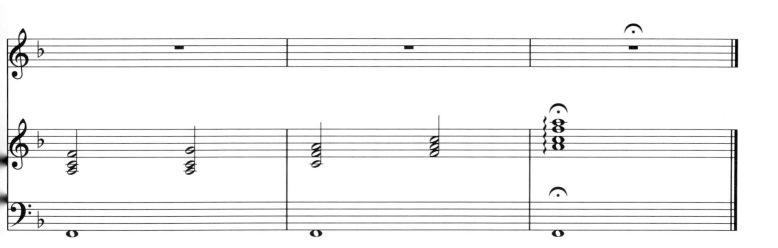

LAVENDER BLUE

(Dilly Dilly)

Words by LARRY MOREY
Music by ELIOT DANIEL

SALUDOS AMIGOS
(From Walt Disney's "THE THREE CABALLEROS")

Words by NED WASHINGTON
Music by CHARLES WOLCOTT

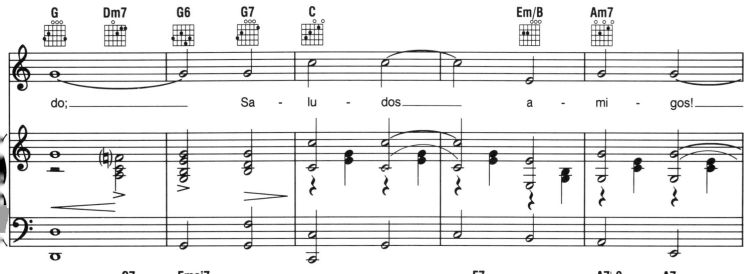

do;_____ Sa - lu - dos____ a - mi - gos!____

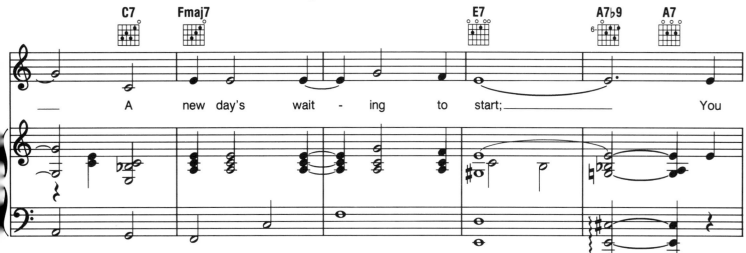

____ A new day's wait - ing to start;_____ You

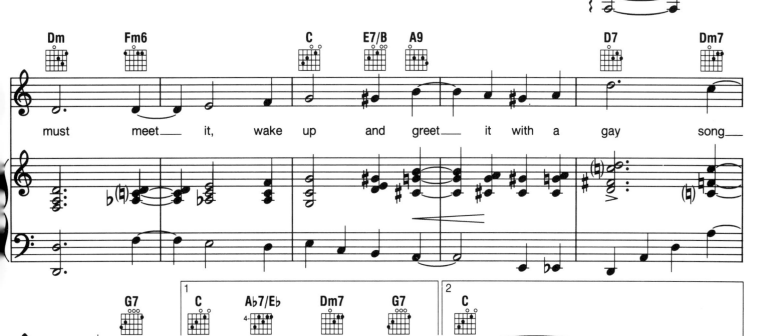

must meet___ it, wake up and greet___ it with a gay song___

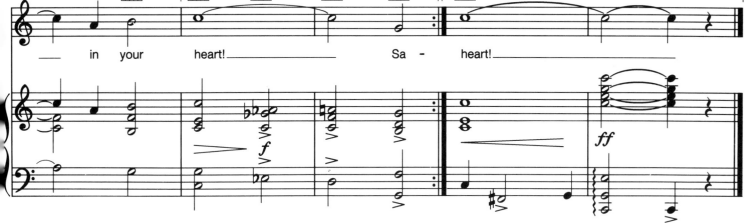

____ in your heart!_____ Sa - heart!_____

THE SECOND STAR TO THE RIGHT

(From Walt Disney's "PETER PAN")

Words by SAMMY CAHN
Music by SAMMY FAIN

Slowly, with expression

The sec - ond star to the right shines in the night for
The sec - ond star to the right shines with a light that's

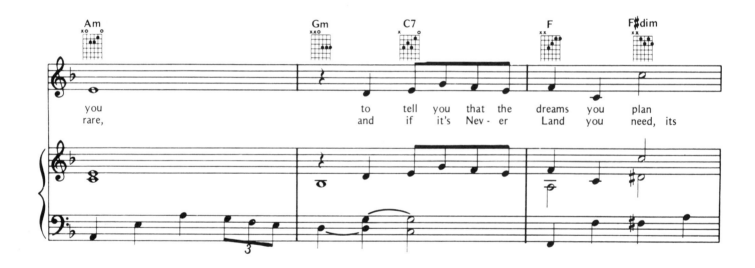

you rare, to and tell you if it's that Nev the - er dreams Land you you plan need, its

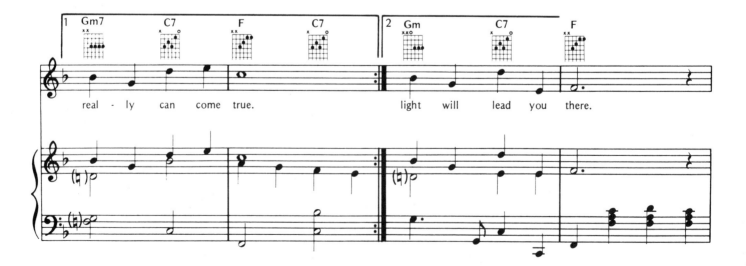

real - ly can come true.

light will lead you there.

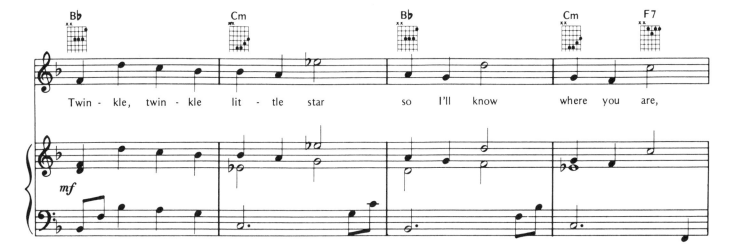

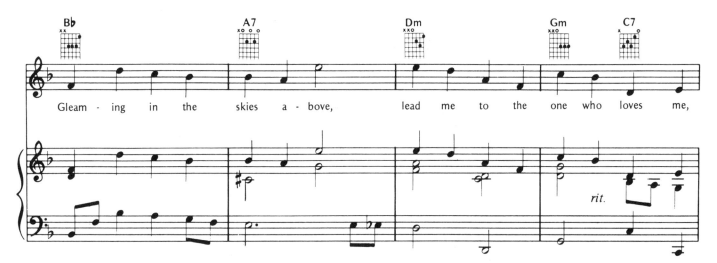

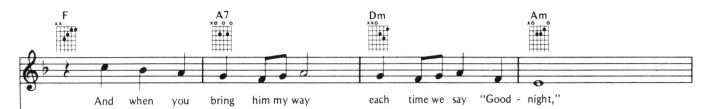

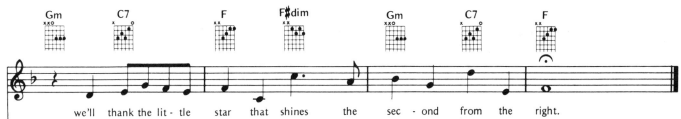

THE SIAMESE CAT SONG

Words and Music by PEGGY LEE
and SONNY BURKE

We are Si - am - ee - iz if you plee - iz,   We are Si - am - ee - iz if you don't please.

We are for - mer res - i - dents of Si - am.   There {is / are} no fin - er cat than {I / we} am.

SO THIS IS LOVE
(From Walt Disney's "CINDERELLA")

Words and Music by
MACK DAVID, AL HOFFMAN
and JERRY LIVINGSTON

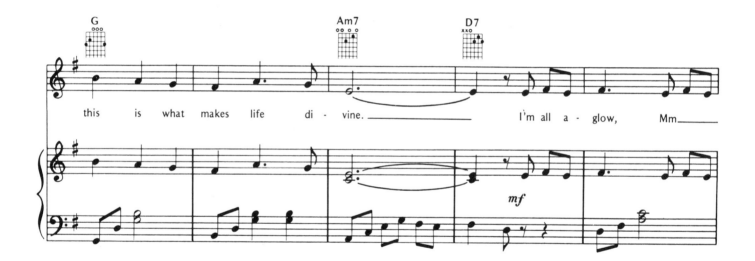

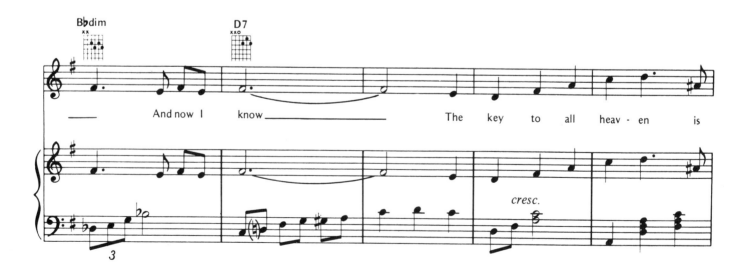

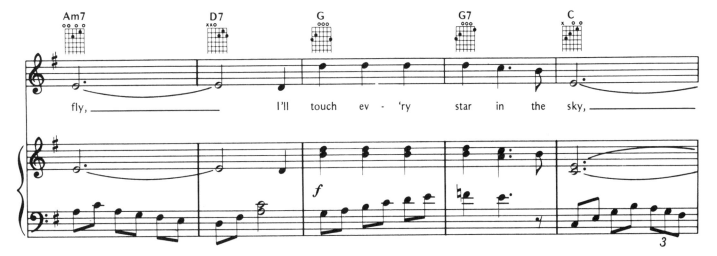

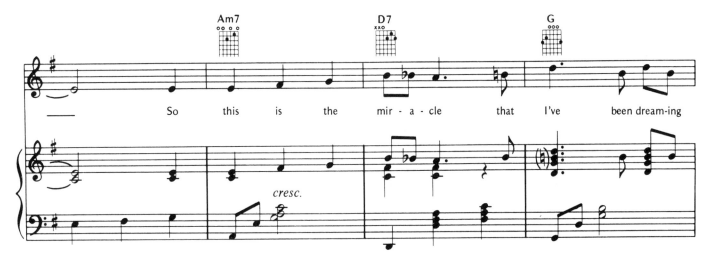

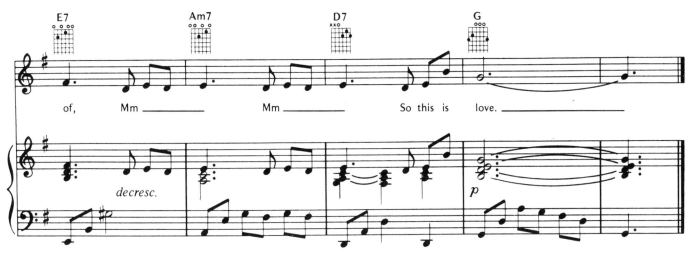

SOME DAY MY PRINCE WILL COME

(From Walt Disney's "SNOW WHITE AND THE SEVEN DWARFS")

Words by LARRY MOREY
Music by FRANK CHURCHILL

Rather fast

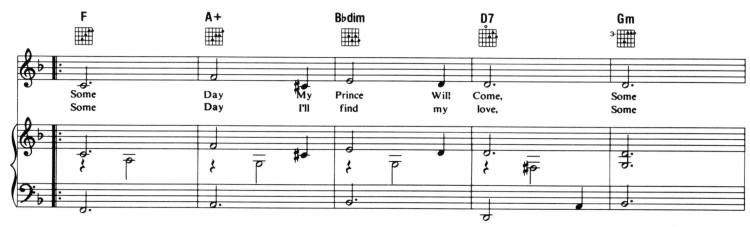

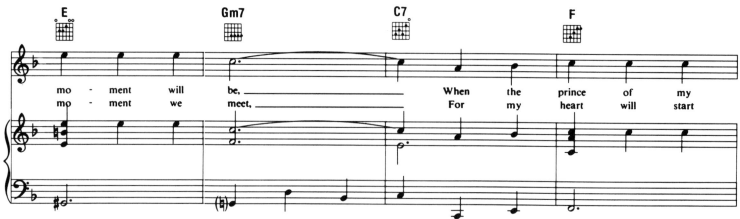

SOMEONE'S WAITING FOR YOU

(From Walt Disney's "THE RESCUERS")

Words by CAROL CONNORS and AYN ROBBINS
Music by SAMMY FAIN

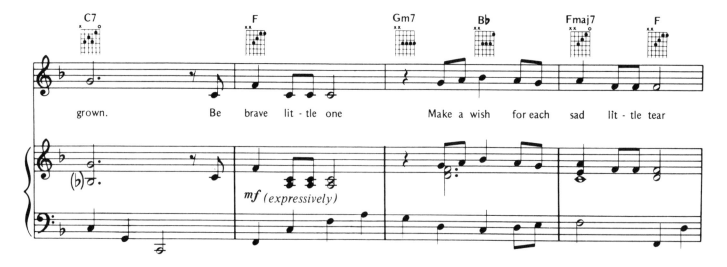

113

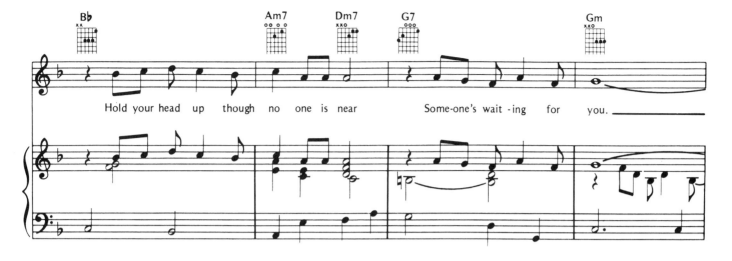

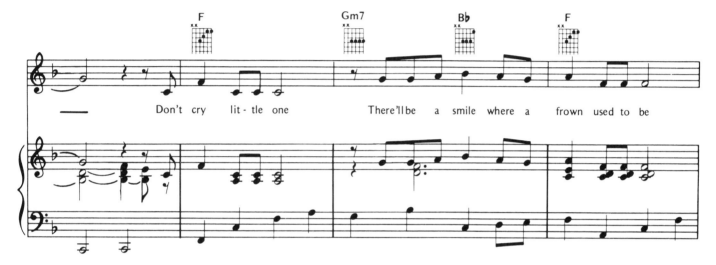

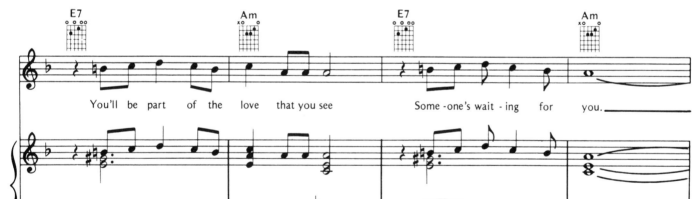

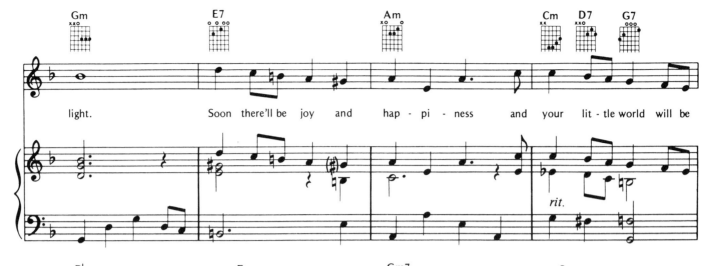

light. Soon there'll be joy and hap-pi-ness and your lit-tle world will be

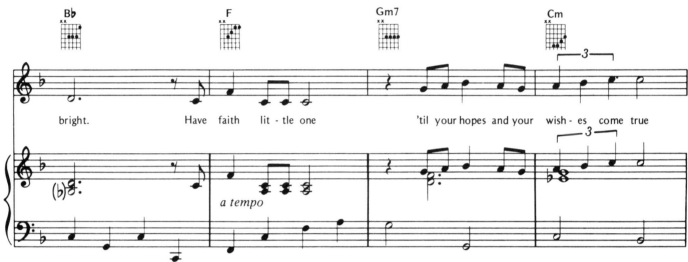

bright. Have faith lit-tle one 'til your hopes and your wish-es come true

You must try to be brave lit-tle one_____ Some-one's wait - ing

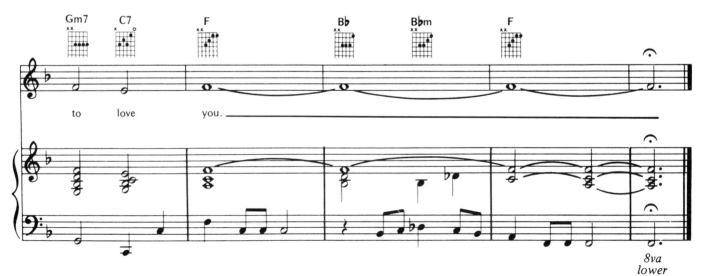

to love you._____

8va lower

A SPOONFUL OF SUGAR

Words and Music by RICHARD M. SHERMAN
and ROBERT B. SHERMAN

In ev - 'ry job that must be done there is an
feath - er - ing his nest has ver - y

el - e - ment of fun; You find the fun and
lit - tle time to rest While gath - er - ing his

snap the job's a game; And ev - 'ry task you un - der -
bits of twine and twig. Though quite in - tent in his pur -

take be - comes a piece of cake, A lark! A
suit he has a mer - ry tune to toot; He knows a

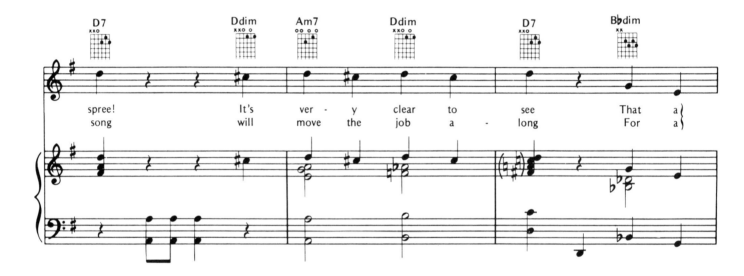

spree! It's ver - y clear to see That a
song will move the job a - long For a

spoon - ful of su - gar helps the med - i - cine go

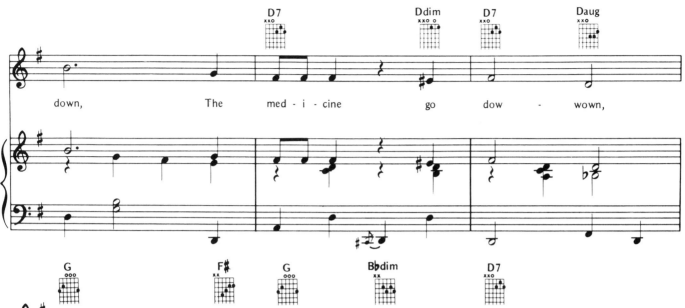

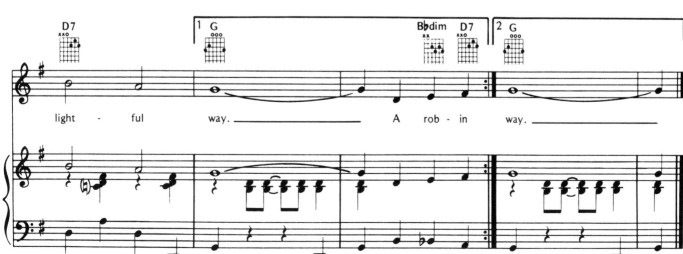

SUPERCALIFRAGILISTICEXPIALIDOCIOUS

(From Walt Disney's "MARY POPPINS")

Words and Music by RICHARD M. SHERMAN
and ROBERT B. SHERMAN

THE TIKI TIKI TIKI ROOM

(From The Disneyland And Walt Disney World Attraction THE ENCHANTED TIKI ROOM)

Words and Music by RICHARD M. SHERMAN
and ROBERT B. SHERMAN

THEME FROM ZORRO

Words by NORMAN FOSTER
Music by GEORGE BRUNS

WHEN YOU WISH UPON A STAR
(From Walt Disney's "PINOCCHIO")

Words by NED WASHINGTON
Music by LEIGH HARLINE

With expression

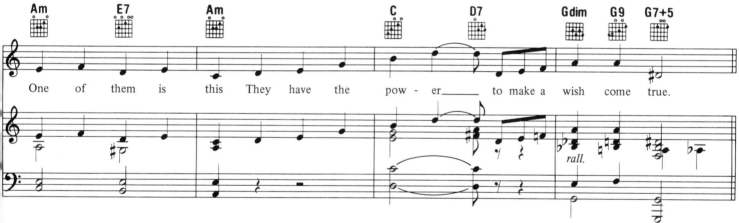

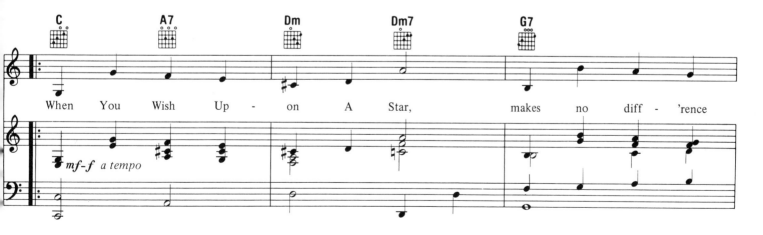

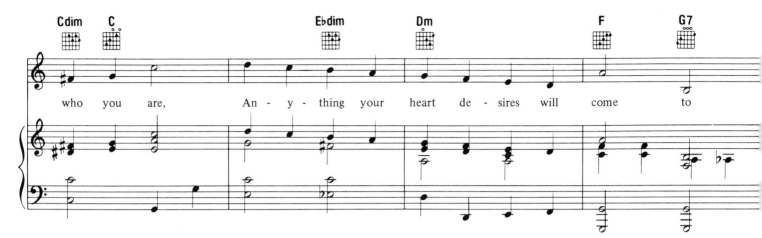

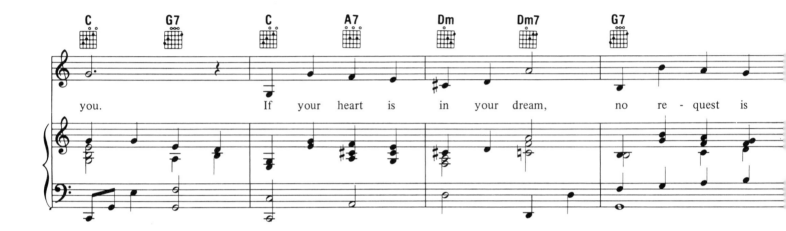

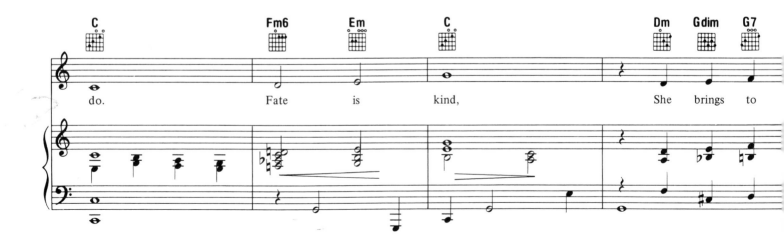

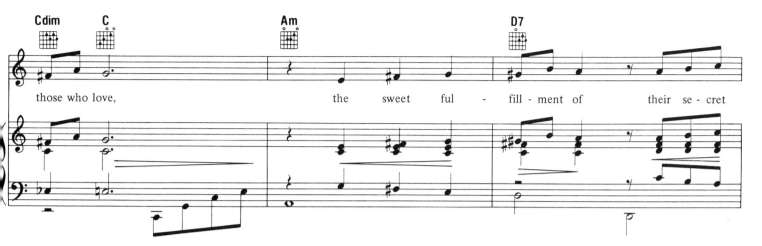

those who love, the sweet ful - fill - ment of their se - cret

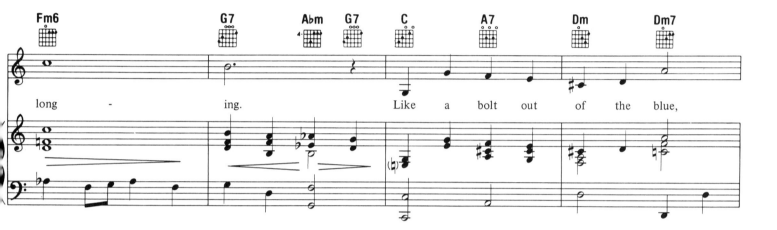

long - ing. Like a bolt out of the blue,

Fate steps in and sees you thru, When You Wish Up - on A Star your

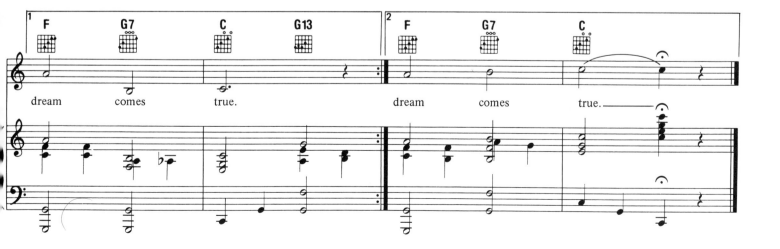

dream comes true. dream comes true.

UNDER THE SEA
(From Walt Disney's "THE LITTLE MERMAID")

Lyrics by HOWARD ASHMAN
Music by ALAN MENKEN

WHEN I SEE AN ELEPHANT FLY
(From "DUMBO")

Words by NED WASHINGTON
Music by OLIVER WALLACE

WHISTLE WHILE YOU WORK
(From Walt Disney's "SNOW WHITE AND THE SEVEN DWARFS")

Words by LARRY MOREY
Music by FRANK CHURCHILL

Brightly

Just whis-tle while you work, (whistle) _____ Put
hum a mer-ry song, (hum) _____ Just

on that grin and start right in to whis-tle loud and long. Just
do your best then take a rest and sing your-self a

WHO'S AFRAID OF THE BIG BAD WOLF?

(From "THE THREE LITTLE PIGS")

Words and Music by FRANK CHURCHILL
Additional Lyric by ANN RONELL

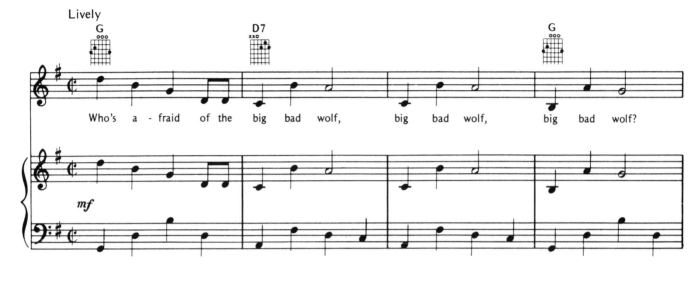

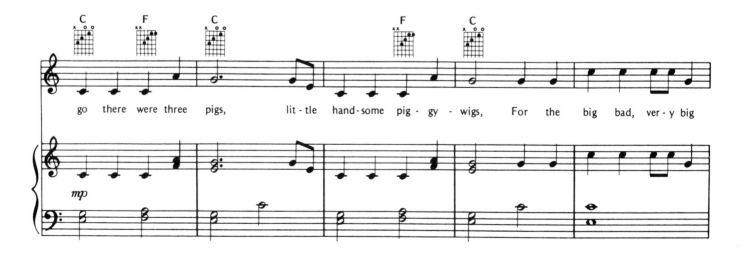

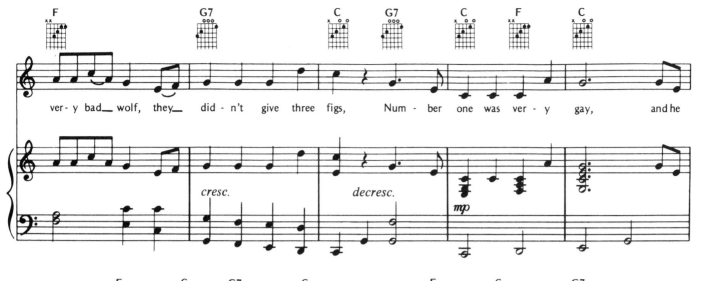

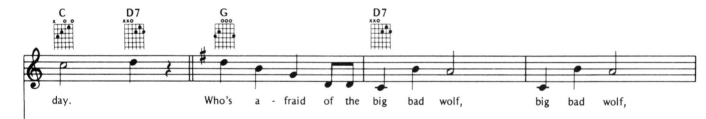

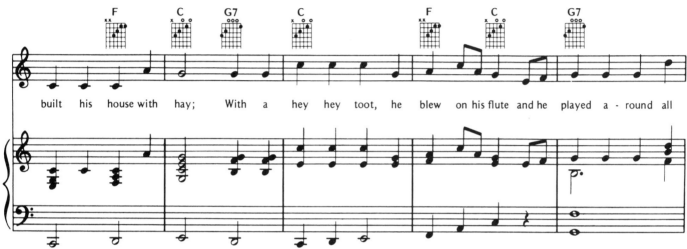

WITH A SMILE AND A SONG

(From Walt Disney's "SNOW WHITE AND THE SEVEN DWARFS")

Words by LARRY MOREY
Music by FRANK CHURCHILL

With a smile and a song,   Life is just like a
With a smile and a song,   All the world seems to

bright sun-ny day,   Your cares fade a-way,____   And your heart   is
wak-en a-new,   Re-joic-ing with you,____   As the song   is

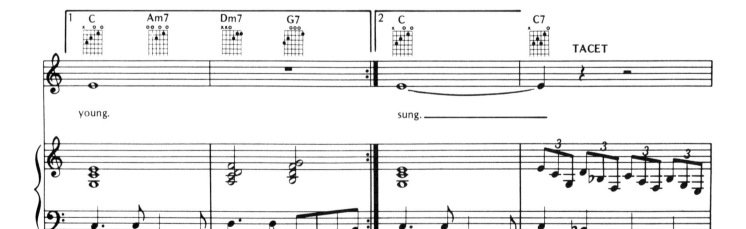

young.
sung.

149

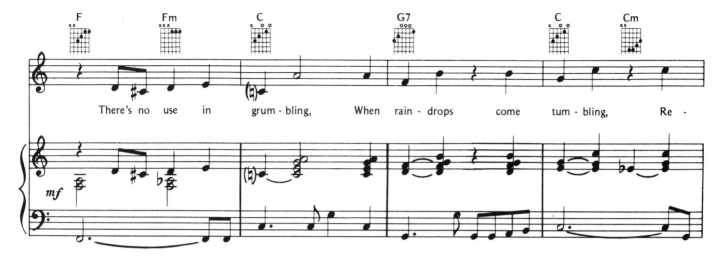

There's no use in grum - bling, When rain - drops come tum - bling, Re -

mem - ber you're the one, Who can fill the world with sun - shine.

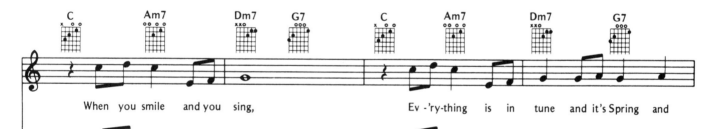

When you smile and you sing, Ev - 'ry-thing is in tune and it's Spring and

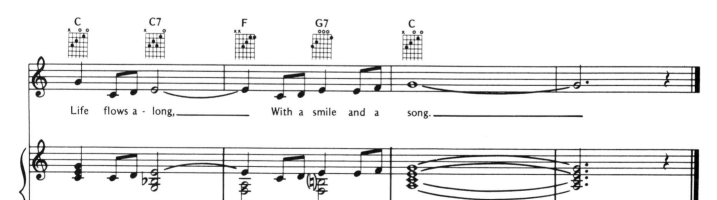

Life flows a - long,_____ With a smile and a song._____

THE WORK SONG

Words and Music by MACK DAVID,
AL HOFFMAN and JERRY LIVINGSTON

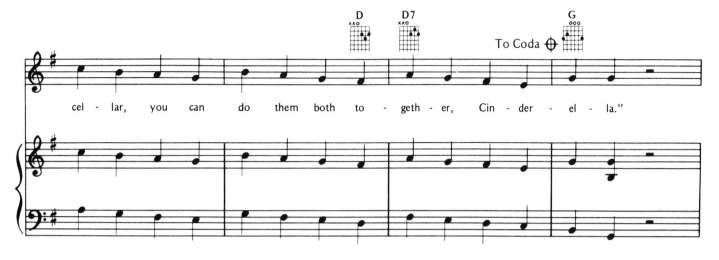

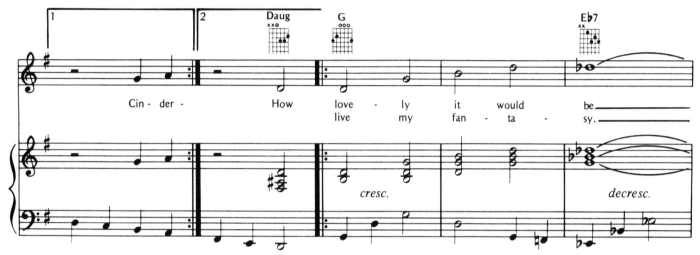

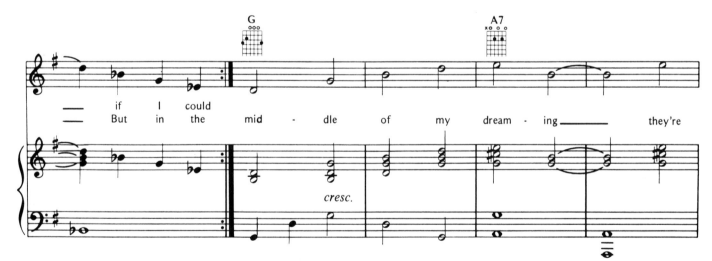

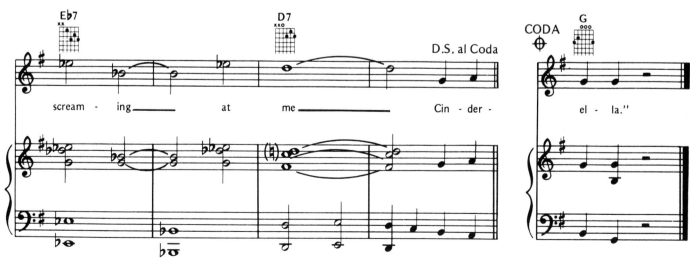

YO, HO
(A PIRATE'S LIFE FOR ME)
(From the Disneyland/Walt Disney World attraction, "Pirates Of The Caribbean")

Words by XAVIER ATENCIO
Music by GEORGE BRUNS

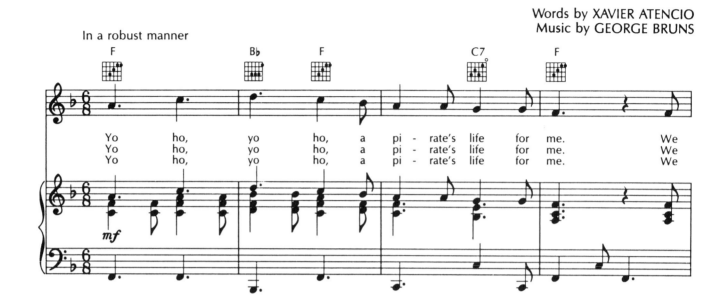

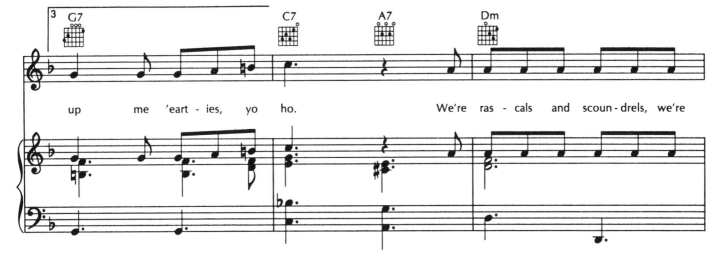

up me 'eart - ies, yo ho. We're ras - cals and scoun - drels, we're

vil - lians and knaves. Drink up me 'eart - ies, yo ho. We're

dev - ils and black sheep, we're real - ly bad eggs. Drink up me 'eart - ies, yo

ho. Yo ho, yo ho, a pi - rate's life for me.

YOU CAN FLY! YOU CAN FLY! YOU CAN FLY!

Words by SAMMY CAHN
Music by SAMMY FAIN

Moderately

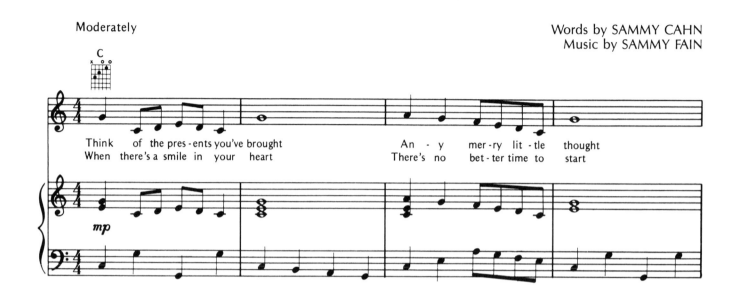

Think of the pres-ents you've brought   An-y mer-ry lit-tle   thought
When there's a smile in your heart   There's no bet-ter time to   start

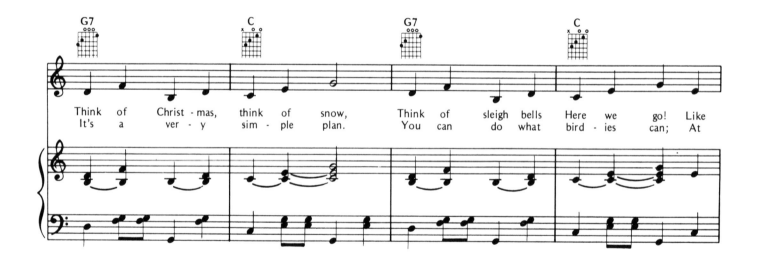

Think of Christ-mas, think of snow,   Think of sleigh bells Here we go! Like
It's a ver-y sim-ple plan.   You can do what bird-ies can; At

rein-deer in the sky_____   You can fly! You can
least it's worth a try_____

To Coda

ZIP-A-DEE-DOO-DAH
(From Walt Disney's "SONG OF THE SOUTH")

Words by RAY GILBERT
Music by ALLIE WRUBEL

Zip - a-dee-doo - dah, Zip - a-dee - ay,_____ My, oh

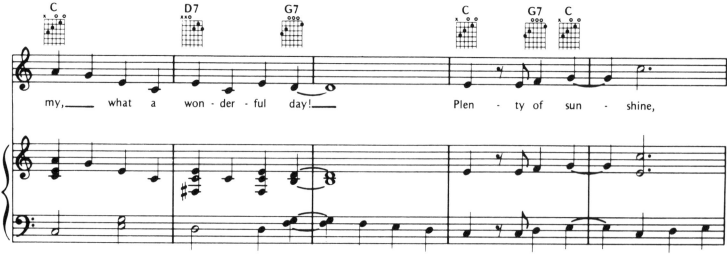

my,_____ what a won-der-ful day!_____ Plen - ty of sun - shine,

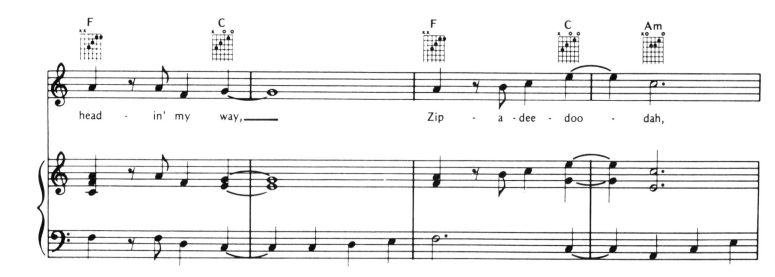

head - in' my way,_____ Zip - a-dee-doo - dah,

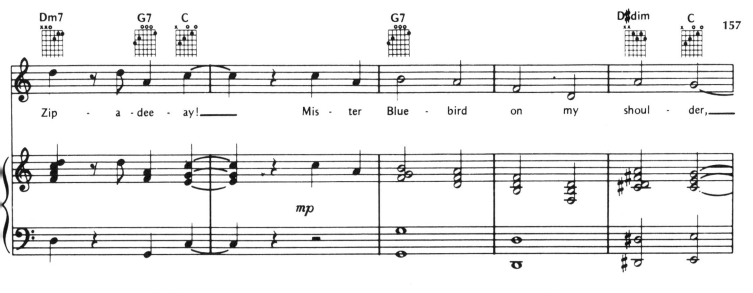

Zip - a - dee - ay!___ Mis - ter Blue - bird on my shoul - der,___

It's the truth, it's "act - ch'll", Ev - 'ry - thing is

TACET

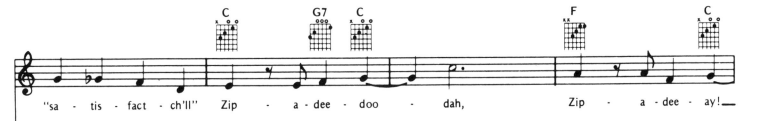

"sa - tis - fact - ch'll" Zip - a - dee - doo - dah, Zip - a - dee - ay!___

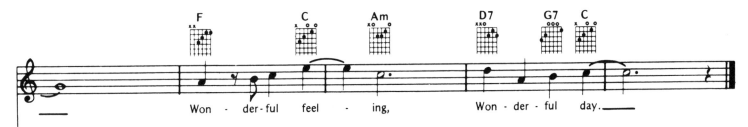

Won - der - ful feel - ing, Won - der - ful day.___

WINNIE THE POOH

Words and Music by RICHARD M. SHERMAN
and ROBERT B. SHERMAN

Tenderly

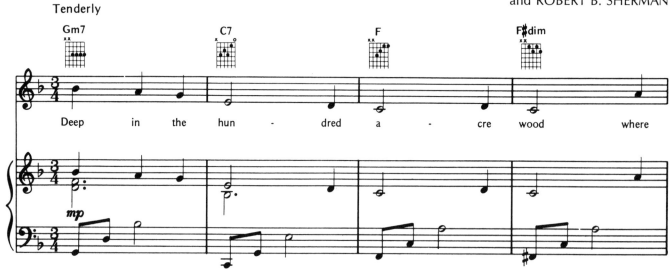

Deep in the hun - dred a - cre wood where

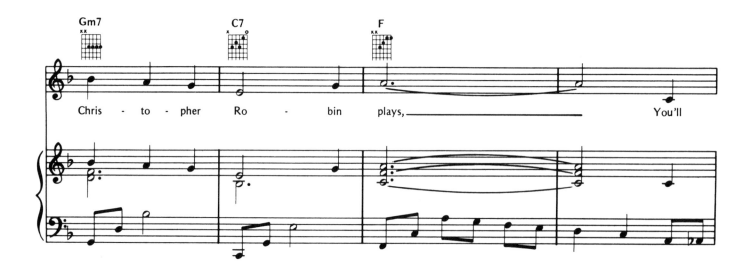

Chris - to - pher Ro - bin plays, _____ You'll

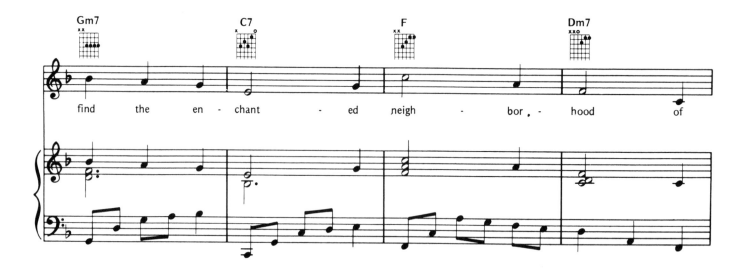

find the en - chant - ed neigh - bor, - hood of

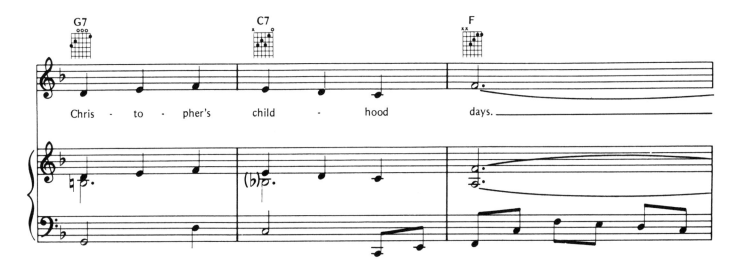

Chris - to - pher's child - hood days._____

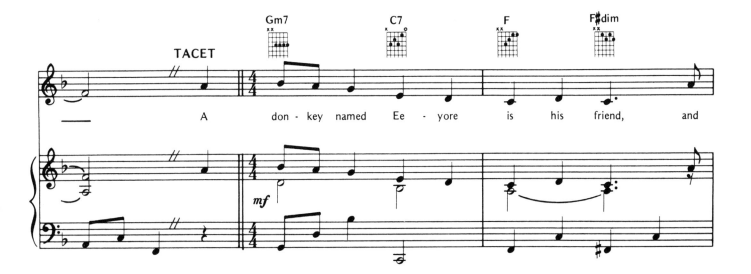

TACET

A don - key named Ee - yore is his friend, and

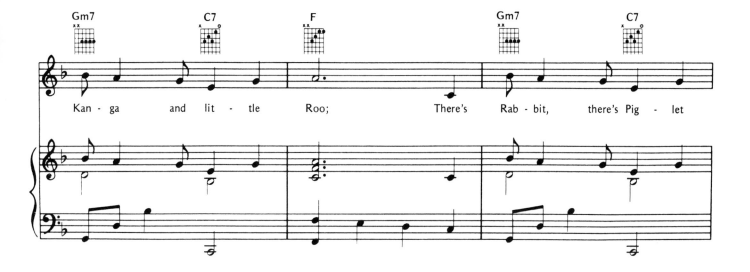

Kan - ga and lit - tle Roo; There's Rab - bit, there's Pig - let

160

and there's Owl, but most of all Win-nie the Pooh!

Win-nie the Pooh, Win-nie the Pooh, tub-by lit-tle cub-by all

stuffed with fluff, He's Win-nie the Pooh, Win-nie the Pooh;

wil-ly, nil-ly, sil-ly ole bear. bear.